C000276665

# William's Christmas Dream

### Linda Carol Morris

Illustrations by
**Frances Espanol**

Copyright © 2021 by Linda Carol Morris. 817155

All rights reserved. No part of this book may be reproduced or transmitted
in any form or by any means, electronic or mechanical, including
photocopying, recording, or by any information storage and retrieval
system, without permission in writing from the copyright owner.

To order additional copies of this book, contact:
Xlibris
UK TFN: 0800 0148620 (Toll Free inside the UK)
UK Local: 02036 956328 (+44 20 3695 6328 from outside the UK)
www.xlibrispublishing.co.uk
Orders@ Xlibrispublishing.co.uk

ISBN:   Softcover      978-1-6641-1395-4
        Hardcover      978-1-6641-1593-4
        EBook          978-1-6641-1394-7

Print information available on the last page

Rev. date: 06/21/2021

For William...

A poem about a boy who has a dream

about a wish...

A gift from Ma-Ma.

It is Christmas Eve

And throughout Tumpton Town

The streets fill with snow

As the darkness comes down

But through a window we spy

William sleeping in his bed

And as the stars fill the sky

Dreams fill his head

He dreams of Santa flying

Through the frosty air

With his galloping reindeer

Racing here, there and everywhere

Their journey is lit

By a huge full moon

As it floats in the sky

Like a giant balloon

The sheep start to shiver

The trees start to freeze

And the tickly snowflakes

Make poor Rudolph sneeze!

He sneezes so hard

That the sleigh spins around

And lands in a forest

Upside-down on the ground!

And all the World's presents

Spill out on the floor

And Rudolph's red nose

Feels very, very sore

But all the other reindeer

Help to straighten the sleigh

And they and Santa

Are soon on their way

They fly over mountains

As high as the sky

Sliding down glaciers

In the blink of an eye

They travel afar

Around the whole wide world

Through blizzards that blind them

And whirl and swirl

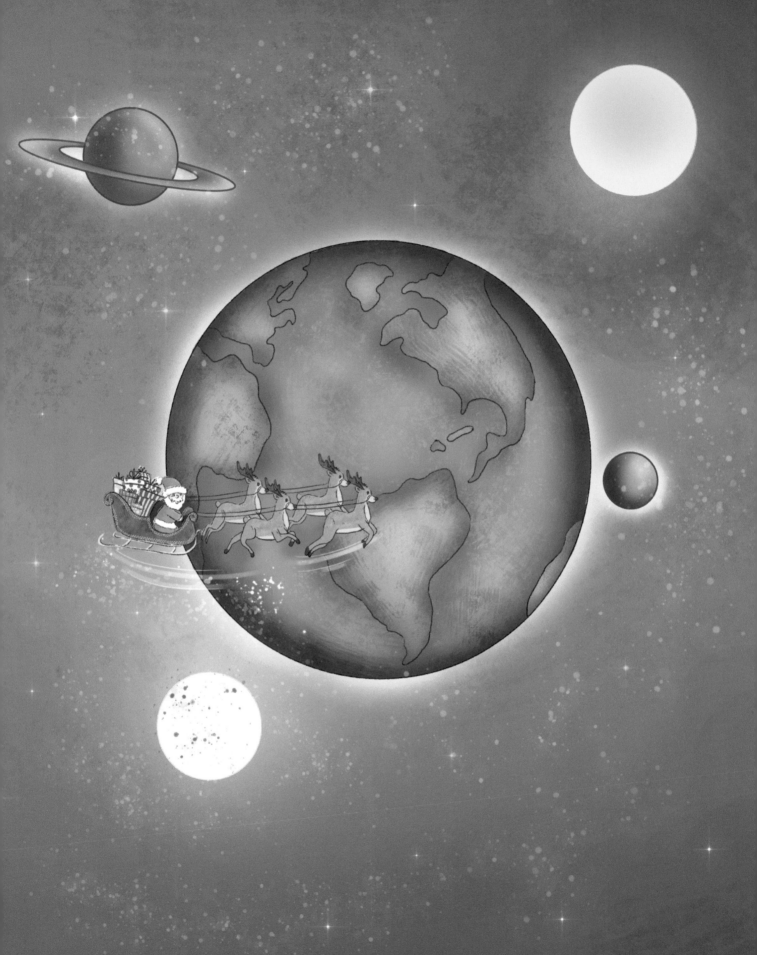

And William dreams

He can see through the keyhole

Santa's mad rush

From North Pole to South Pole

And the bells ring out

In the night so clear

Telling the world

That Christmas is here

They tell young William

Why we celebrate Christmas

Why we give to others

With our hearts full of goodness

It's to remember a baby

Born far away

Under a star that shone

On the manger where he lay

Three Kings from the East

Brought gifts for the boy

Whose birthday they celebrate

With wonder and joy

Even the animals

Know that Christmas is here

The donkeys, the sheep

The goats and the deer

They all lift their heads

To see the stars in the sky

And remember that first Christmas...

Then Santa whizzes by!

William crosses his fingers

And crosses his toes

That Santa will reach him

But so HARD the wind blows!

He says 'I can't wait

For Santa to come'

With the pearly white bracelet

My gift for my Mum

I know that my Dad

Would like some socks

Some with stripes

And some with spots

And for my lovely dog Tessa

A bone to crunch

So she can join in the fun

When we eat our lunch"

On Christmas Day

When William wakes from his dreaming

He rushes downstairs

To see his Mum and Dad beaming

They hug him and kiss him

Their kind little boy

Who thought not of himself

But of others' joy

The End

Lightning Source UK Ltd.
Milton Keynes UK
UKHW050903060222
398186UK00006B/92